A Squirrel's Dilemma Coloring Book

Through Life, we All Lose Something

Arthur Peter Martin Bieri

AuthorHouse™
1663 Liberty Drive
Bloomington, IN 47403
www.authorhouse.com
Phone: 833-262-8899

This book is printed on acid-free paper.

ISBN: 978-1-6655-7752-6 (sc)
ISBN: 978-1-6655-7753-3 (e)

Print information available on the last page.

Published by AuthorHouse 03/30/2023

authorHOUSE®

Dedication

To my invaluable family, past and present, my family is my pride and happiness.

To Authorhouse colleagues for their professional guidance and arrangement of "A Squirrel's Dilemma."

To all the squirrels in heaven who didn't make it across the street.

To my illustrator, Walt Sumner for his untiring efforts toward "A Squirrel's Dilemma."

About The Book

Progress may be good, but progress will be an adjustment. When a change involves a change in living and uprooting of surroundings, it's major.

This book is about progress, "a squirrel's dilemma", and adjustment. About taking down beautiful trees full of pecan nuts in a park area. The park area provided food, shelter, play and sleep for the squirrels as well as safety.

As trees were plowed down and taken away, squirrels scampered to other locations in areas of distance from their habitat.

As days went on, only one tree stump was left shadowed by the barren land.

A squirrel was sitting on that tree stump eating one remaining nut. It was then I thought of "A Squirrel's Dilemma".

A general theme is that when something happens, decisions must be made and adjustments narrowed and the best choice made with comfort.

This is an account of one squirrel's dilemma.

One day when driving through a park area, I stopped and watched squirrels playing on the ground, jumping from tree branches and limbs back to trees.

The squirrels were gathering nature's food of nuts and seeds.

I watched and watched, then
I left the park area.

The next day I returned watching the squirrels in the same park.

From a short distance, I saw bulldozers, dump trucks, and heavy equipment in the park.

The squirrels' "chirr", — sounds began to disband the major population of squirrels in the park.

The squirrels went scampering away.

The next day, the equipment and workers caught my attention and I saw many downed trees, trees that the squirrels had used, jumping from branch to limbs and limbs to tree branches.

Bulldozers, trucks, and workers took the squirrels' playground.

The trees that were a place of safety, their homes, feeding locations, areas to hide and sleep, had fallen— fallen. Trees were lying everywhere.

But one tree still stood
tall, full of nuts.

On the ground were nuts, berries, mushrooms, and seeds. Few squirrels were around it.

It was the last tree standing. It was a tall tree with a large base, large branches and few squirrels eating and gathering food.

The next day, the trees were taken away.

some stumps remained.

Then there was one tree stump.

One squirrel was sitting on the last tree stump. With a nut in his front feet, staring, chirr—

The squirrel's dilemma.

Through life, we all lose something.

ACHIEVEMENTS AND OTHER WORKS

Contemporary Authors, volumes 61-64, "A Bibliographical Guide to Current Authors and Their works", Gale Research Co., 1976.

"A Practical Guide for the Teaching of Physical Education in the Still water Public Schools", 1962.

"How we Do It Game Book" Contributed Games - AAHPR, 1201 16th St., N.W. Washington, D.C. 20036 - 1964.

"Action Games" - Fearson Publishers/Lear Siegler, Inc. - Education Division, Belmont, California 94002. 1972 - 1st Printing, Sept., 1999 - 2nd Printing, 2016 - 3rd Printing.

"A Swimming Program for the Handicapped" -Association Press, NY, with Colleagues, 1973.

"A Practical Guide for Teaching the Mentally Retarded to Swim", with Colleagues, 1969 for The Kennedy Foundation.

"Outstanding Young Men of America" 1967 Edition, P.O. Box 3396, Montgomery, Alabama 36109

"Personalities of The South", A publication of News Publishers Co. Inc.

Suite206, 7 - Lawyers Bldg. P.O. Box 226 Raleigh, North Carolina 27602

"Guest Author" A Directory of Speakers - Hermes Press, 51 Lenox Street, Brocton, Mass. 02401

When one reads "A Squirrel's Dilemma" Through Life, we All Lose Something. What brings comfort is that spring will come again and there is hope.

Printed in the United States
by Baker & Taylor Publisher Services